dwarf hamsters

understanding and
caring for your pet

D0307830

Written by
Dr Anne McBride BSc PhD Cert.Cons FRSA

dwarf hamsters

understanding and
caring for your pet

Written by
Dr Anne McBride BSc PhD Cert.Cons FRSA

Magnet & Steel Ltd

www.magnetsteel.com

Every reasonable care has been taken in the compilation of this publication. The Publisher and Author cannot accept liability for any loss, damage, injury or death resulting from the keeping of dwarf hamsters by user(s) of this publication, or from the use of any materials, equipment, methods or information recommended in this publication or from any errors or omissions that may be found in the text of this publication or that may occur at a future date, except as expressly provided by law.

No animals were harmed in the making of this book.

The 'he' pronoun is used throughout this book instead of the rather impersonal 'it', however no gender bias is intended.

Printed and bound in South Korea.

ISBN: 978-1-907337-06-2
ISBN: 1-907337-06-7

Contents

Perfect pets

Dwarf hamsters have been popular pets since the 1970s. There are four species of dwarf hamster and this book will tell you about them, so you can choose which type you want and learn how to keep them.

There are several reasons why they are attractive animals to keep:

- If treated gently, dwarf hamsters rarely bite and like to interact with their owners.

- Dwarf hamsters are not expensive to buy or to keep.

- Dwarf hamsters are clean creatures and, providing they are kept well, they are not smelly animals.

- Dwarf hamsters, as their name suggests are very small. They range in size from the tiny Roborovski which weighs between 20 and 25 g (0.7- 0.9 oz) to the larger Campbell's Russian hamster, which still only weighs 30 to 50 g (1.05- 1.7 oz). As a consequence of their size they do not need a lot of space, compared to other pet animals such as rabbits, guinea pigs, dogs and cats.

- Dwarf hamsters come in a range of different colours.

- They are active, busy creatures and are fun to watch.

- Dwarf hamsters live for around 2 years.

Dwarf hamsters enjoy a variety of foods including sunflower seeds.

Special needs

Dwarf hamsters are delightful creatures, with their cute bodies and lively and inquisitive natures. But, like all animals, they have their own special requirements which you need to know about before buying your first hamsters.

This is important so you can have a good relationship with your hamsters, and they can live long, healthy and happy lives. Also, in the UK, you now have a legal obligation to ensure your pet is healthy and happy.

If you are buying a hamster for a child, please remember that it is still the adult's responsibility to ensure the hamster is well cared for and properly handled. Indeed, as these animals are so tiny and quick to move, it is strongly recommended that they are not bought for young children, who may accidentally squeeze them or drop them. Rather, they should be considered as a pet for older children and adults.

Hamsters bond well with humans, but must be handled gently as they are tiny and easily frightened.

Points to remember

- You will need to handle your hamsters gently, as they are easily frightened, especially when picked up. For this reason, young children, especially under the age of seven, should be supervised when handling dwarf hamsters.

- You need to give your hamsters the right food to keep them fit and healthy.

- You will need to clean out your hamsters' home regularly.

- You will need to provide a cage that is large enough for proper exercise. Hamsters are very energetic and must have appropriate things to do to keep them occupied.

- Dwarf hamsters are most active at night, and find bright lights and noise distressing.

- You will need to make arrangements for someone to look after your hamsters if you go away on holiday.

- You will need to give your hamsters a weekly check to ensure they are healthy.

- You will need to commit to looking after your hamster throughout its life, which may be 2 years or more.

Hamsters are omnivores and love variety in their diet – different textures of food help to erode their constantly growing teeth.

What is a dwarf hamster?

Hamsters are members of the rodent family. This is the largest group of mammals, and contains over 2,000 different species of varying sizes and shapes. The word rodent comes from the Latin word 'rodere', meaning to gnaw, and gnawing is one thing all rodents have in common.

They gnaw to get their food and to make their homes. Rodents have four big front teeth, the incisors, that have evolved for gnawing. These sharp chisel-shaped teeth meet together like pincers and are very effective. They grow continually throughout the animal's life.

There are over 50 species and subspecies of hamster in the world. There are four species of dwarf hamster that are kept as pets. These are the Chinese, the Roborovski, and Russian or Djungarian which is comprised of two close related types, known as sub-species the Winter White Russian (or more correctly Siberian Winter White) and Campbell's Russian. These 'Russian' hamsters are also known as 'Furry Footed'. Dwarf hamsters have a well-known cousin, the Syrian or Golden hamster, which you may also see in the pet shop. However, each species is different and this book is only concerned with the four types of dwarf hamster.

Hamsters belong to a family of rodents called the Myomorpha, which also includes mice, rats, gerbils, lemmings and voles. The word hamster comes from the German word 'hamstern' meaning to hoard. This very accurately describes a major behaviour of these animals.

In this section you can learn about where dwarf hamsters come from and how they spend their time in the wild.

Dwarf hamsters, as their name suggests, are very small creatures. They are between 67-127 mm (2.6 - 5 inches) long from nose to beginning of the tail, depending on species. The Chinese is the largest.

It is important to realise that all hamsters are prey animals and are a major source of food for many meat-eating animals (predators). They are hunted on the ground by animals and from the air by birds. This has an effect on everything they do and explains why they are continually on the alert and appear very nervous.

Hamsters are very adept at spotting danger. They have excellent hearing and sense of smell and, while quite short sighted, the position of their eyes means they can see above as well as behind them. They run to safety at the first sign of any danger, and can be very quick, reaching speeds of 8 km (5 miles) an hour.

Dwarf hamsters are exceptionally busy and active animals. They can travel long distances in their search for food and bedding material. As with many small prey species, such as mice and rats, they are active at night. They come out of their nests to search for food and explore their world, clean their sleeping area and make a new nest, or make any repairs to their homes that are needed. They are very curious creatures and will climb over rocks, dig tunnels and gather food in their specially adapted mouths.

Pictured: Hamsters carry food in their mouth pouches, taking it back to their burrows to eat later.

The hamster's mouth has cheek pouches that extend along the jaw, almost back to the shoulders. They are lubricated by mucus which enables the hamster to push food along to the back, a bit like you filling up your shopping bag. They can carry almost half their own body weight in these pouches.

They gather food and nesting material and carry it back in their strong mouth pouches to the safety of their burrow. Hamsters store their food in a pile from which they can eat later in peace and safety. They are omnivores, which means their natural diet includes meat, in the form of insects and grubs, as well as seeds, nuts and fruit.

In the wild dwarf hamsters are regarded as agricultural pests. They are identified by their official Latin names, which are almost as long as the animals! These names are unique to each species or sub species, and indicate how closely related they may be. For example, the two Russian and the Roborovski hamsters all share the first name of Phodopus (meaning short-tailed), showing they all belong to the same group. But the Chinese dwarf hamster's first name is Cricetulus, showing it belongs in the group of long-tailed hamsters.

All four species come from Central Asia, a landscape of mountains, grassland and semi-desert known as

Pictured: As prey animals, dwarf hamsters need safe places in which to hide. They venture out morning and evening when it is safe.

the Steppes. However, each has its own particular type of habitat for which it is specially adapted. They all have their own way of making homes to keep them safe from predators, warm in the winter and cool in the summer, as they can quickly overheat and will die at temperatures of 36°C (97°F).

The Winter White Russian (Phodopus sungorus sungorus) and its very close relative the Campbell's Russian (Phodopus sungorus campbellii) both originate from grasslands, though they will also live in more rocky or sandy areas. The Winter White is so called because it lives in more northerly areas that are covered by snow in winter. It changes its coat colour from brown to white as the days shorten.

Like the Golden or Syrian, these Russian hamsters are engineers, constructing underground burrows in which to keep safe and warm. The burrows are not as complicated or as large as those of the Golden hamster, but are still impressive feats for such tiny animals. The Russian hamster's home is a long burrow, often as deep as a metre (3 feet) with a nest at the end and other tunnels and chambers sometimes leading almost vertically upwards to the main entrance. The Russians cousin, the Roborovski hamster (Phodopus roborovskii), also makes a burrow for its home. However, as it lives in sandy desert areas, tunnels are more prone to collapse, so it makes a simpler straight single tunnel with its nest at the end. The Chinese hamster (Cricetulus griseus) does not often make burrows. It lives in rocky areas where digging is difficult, and it makes its shelters in the cracks and crevices between the rocks or in caves.

Because the burrows are well below ground the temperature inside stays very much the same, enabling the animals to keep cool in the summer and warm in the winter. Hamsters are very tidy creatures and will use different parts of their burrow or shelter system for different activities. One part will be used as a latrine (toilet), another for their food larder and another for their sleeping and resting area, where they will spend long periods of time grooming their coat as well as sleeping. A female will use yet another part as a nursery for her babies.

In the wild, hamsters have their young in the late spring and summer, when food is plentiful. Pregnancy is between 16 and 20 days, depending on the species. A female Roborovski will have up to 4 babies in a litter, whereas the larger Chinese usually has 6 or 7, but has been known to have as many as 12! Baby hamsters are born hairless and their eyes and ears are closed, so they do not see or hear. They do, however, have a set of sharp teeth when they are born. Their ears open when they are about 4 days old and the eyes at about 2 weeks. The hair begins to grow in the first week after birth.

At this stage they are totally dependent on their mother to keep them fed, warm and protected. They start to eat solid food and drink water when they are about 10 days old and weaning begins around 3 weeks, when the mother starts to leave them to look after themselves for periods of time by making a separate nest to sleep in. Around 2 weeks of age the babies start to play fight, pinning each other down and attacking each other's heads, rushing around playing and exploring their home. They are able to be fully separated from their mother when 5 weeks old.

Pictured: Building trust with a hamster is very rewarding.

The human link

The history of the relationship between hamsters and humans is fascinating and unusual. The first hamster species to be brought into captivity was the Golden or Syrian hamster and this was a popular pet from the middle of the 20th century.

The dwarf hamsters' popularity as pets did not start until quite a bit later. The first to enter captivity was the Campbell, arriving in the UK in 1964, soon followed by the Winter White Russian hamsters, the first 4 being caught from the wild in Western Siberia in 1968. The Chinese hamster was also seen in captivity around the same period, though originally used as research animals in scientific institutions. It wasn't until 1982 that the first Roborovski hamsters were seen, brought in from Germany by a hamster fancier.

Since their introduction as pets, many different varieties have been bred by those interested in showing these animals. The first organisation for hamster 'fanciers' was the National Hamster Council, formed in Britain in 1949. Nowadays there are hamster shows held all over the country.

Pictured: Removing the edible kernel from sunflower seeds.

The hamster's world

Find out how a hamster functions and how it sees the world.

Nose

Hamsters rely on smell to identify each other, find food, and to detect the scent of a nearby predator. They can recognize other hamsters and different people just by scent.

Whiskers

These are extremely sensitive and are used to help the hamster find its way in the dark and as a measure to decide whether it can fit through a space or if the ground drops away in front of it. The hamster is unique in the mobility of its whiskers. When the hamster is resting, they are flat and

Pictured: Two alert hamsters, with raised whiskers.

still. When alert the whiskers remain still, but are raised to stick out from its face. However, when the hamster is exploring or investigating some new object, the whiskers sweep back and forth.

Mouth

The hamster's mouth has large cheek pouches used for carrying food and bedding material back to its burrow.

Teeth

Hamsters have 16 teeth that grow continually and need to be worn down if it is not to suffer from painful dental conditions. They need to be given the right food and appropriate things to gnaw, such as untreated fruit tree wood.

Eyes

Hamsters have panoramic vision, seeing behind them, to the sides and above their head, but not right in front of the nose. Their eyes are adapted for seeing at twilight and night when light levels are low. Bright light, such as sunshine and electric lights, are painful to hamsters. Hamsters are very short sighted, so it is best to talk to them gently when you approach them so as to not startle them. If you do startle them, they may bite because they are afraid. Hamsters have red or black eyes.

Pictured: Babies need protecting, and hamsters are always looking out for danger.

Ears

Like other rodents, hamsters hear far better than we do. They can hear high-pitched sounds which we cannot, in the ultra-sonic range. This means they hear noises from electronic equipment such as TVs and refrigerators. For hamsters these are very loud and stressful so they will need to live in a quiet place in your home.

Feet

The front feet have four claws (nails) and there are five on the back feet. The soles of the feet of the Campbell and Winter White hamsters are slightly furred to help protect them from the winter cold. Whether furred or bare, all hamsters have feet that are very sensitive, like our hands and fingers. The front toes are used for holding food, gripping surfaces as they climb and for grooming their coat.

Movement

Hamsters walk, trot and run. They can squeeze through narrow gaps – if their head can get through then so can the rest of their body. They are great escapologists!

Tail

The Chinese hamster has a longer tail than the three other species, which it uses use to help it balance when climbing or standing up on its back legs. The Chinese hamster is a much more agile climber than its Russian cousins, due in part to its longer tail.

Body

The body is compact and rounded, with strong muscles on the hips and shoulders.

Coat

The coat is short, though that of the Campbell's is somewhat thicker than the other dwarf hamsters. Each species has its own particular markings and colour.

Colours & marking

Coat colours are divided into three types: agouti, self coloured and patterned. Agouti means wild-type markings and colour, self-coloured refers to a coat of a single colour and patterned to spots or other markings.

Winter White Russian

The natural colour of the White Winter Russian is grey-brown on the back, with a wide dark stripe running along the centre of its back from nose to tail, known as a dorsal stripe. The belly is a paler grey or white, with a darker undercoat. This is perfect camouflage as it trots through moonlit grass, and merges in the shadows cast by the stems of the vegetation. However, in the winter it would be very obvious as a dark blob against the snow and as the daylight shortens in the autumn it replaces its summer coat with one of white. This does not happen when it is kept indoors as the artificial light does not trigger the coat change.

Due to selective breeding Winter White Russians also come in different colours. These range from a pale grey-white, known as pearl, to blue shades, yellows, browns and darker shades that are almost black. The list of colours is: cream, pearl, blue, sapphire, yellow blue fawn, argente (a yellow-light brown colour), mandarin, camel, merle and umbrous. These all retain the dorsal stripe to some extent, though in some, such as the sandy-orange coloured mandarin, it is only a subtle shade darker than the rest of the coat.

Pictured: A white Russian and an Agouti.

Campbell's Russian

The natural colour pattern of the Campbell's Russian is not dissimilar to the summer coat of the Winter White Russian, but reflects differences in the natural habitat. The Campbell is a more yellow-brown colour on top, enabling it to be more camouflaged in the drier habitat of its home in the easterly Steppes of Northern Mongolia and China. Its dorsal stripe is thinner and more sharply-defined than its cousin.

The Campbell's Russian is a favourite in the show world as it has been possible to breed a wider variety of coat colours and textures than the other dwarf hamster species. As well as varieties such as argente, Campbells come in chocolate, black, lilac, dark grey and albino. They can also be mottled in colour where the basic coat is white with delightful coloured splodges.

Campbells are the only dwarf hamsters to have different coat textures. There is the somewhat thick normal coat, and also the satin, which has a sheen to it due to the hair strands being thinner and having more air pockets than normal hamster hair, creating a more reflective surface. Finally rex-coated Campbell's hamsters have been bred with the coat more sparse and wavy. Even the whiskers are slightly wavy.

Campbells and Winter White Russians are sometimes inter-bred, though this has produced offspring with health problems. They are sometimes more aggressive too, inter-breeding is not recommended.

Pictured: An inquisitive Campbell's Russian. hamster.

Roborovski

The Roborovski is seldom seen for sale, due to it being more difficult to breed. It is yellow-brown on its back, with a grey undercoat and, unlike the other species, does not have a dorsal stripe. Its underbelly is white. It is the smallest of the four species, but it has enormous whiskers and round, deep black eyes with pale eyebrows.

Chinese

The largest of the dwarf hamsters, the Chinese is less rounded in shape and has a longer, more obvious tail. Its natural colour is grey-brown with fine black spots of hair, known as 'ticking', similar to the colour of a wild rabbit. It has a black dorsal stripe and grey-white underbelly. Its ears are dark, edged with white, which, with its large black eyes, give it an appearance of being somewhat startled by the world.

There are some variations in colour, notably the spotted and white. However, these are not often seen, as both mutations have problems. White males are sterile and spotted offspring are often born dead.

One hamster or two?

Not a totally simple answer here.
It rather depends on the species.

Winter Whites, Roborovski and Campbells are all sociable species and should be kept with at least one other of their own species. As hamsters will breed easily they should be kept in same-sex groups, so keep the males in a different cage from the females. If your hamsters have lived together since they were young they should get along just fine, so long as they have plenty of space.

Chinese hamsters, while friendly to people are rather less sociable to each other. Indeed they can be very aggressive and it is advised that they are kept alone. Two males or more may live together peaceably if they have lots of space and have been together from a young age, but even this cannot be a guarantee that fierce fighting will not occur when they reach adulthood. Females are less tolerant of company and are probably better living alone.

Do think very carefully before you consider keeping males and females together, as they will inevitably breed. Would you be able to find suitable homes for all the babies? Do you have the specialist knowledge required? If you do find that you seriously want to breed and /or show your hamsters, then you should find out more by contacting the hamster associations in the further information section.

Most dwarf hamsters are sociable, but only same sex hamsters should be kept together as pets.

Setting up home

Before you buy your hamsters, you will need to decide where you are going to keep them. Then buy suitable housing and get it ready before you bring your pet home.

Hamsters do not tolerate heat and should be kept away from sunny windows and radiators and, of course, draughts. Ideally the room temperature should be between 18 - 26°C (65-79°F).

- Your hamster's home should be as big as possible. They are very active and like space to run around and explore. The accommodation will need to contain a dark, draught-free sleeping area.

- You can buy specially-made cages; the most common types have bars on the sides and top. You can attach toys and a wheel to these as well as shelves for your hamster to climb on. Do not buy cages with wire floors or wire shelves, as these can hurt your hamster's feet.

You can also buy modular cages, with tunnels that inter-connect, rather like a hamster's burrow. These need to have adequate ventilation in the tunnels. You can have fun adding to your hamster's home with new tunnels or changing their arrangement, giving your pet new routes to explore.

- The bottom of the cage should be covered with at least 5 cm (2 ins) of litter. This allows your hamsters to dig, and soaks up any mess.

- Suitable materials for digging, burrowing and bedding should be paper-based, such as shredded tissue paper or paper towels, or torn up paper and newspaper.

- Meadow hay is also excellent bedding material especially if combined with shredded paper.

Wood shavings and sawdust are easily available and cheap, but not advised as they may contain chemicals and dust that can cause respiratory problems for your hamster. Other dusty materials, such as cat litter, should also be avoided.

Fibrous materials such as cotton wool or wood wool should not be used. They can easily cause injury to your hamster by getting tangled around feet or teeth or, if swallowed, they may cause impaction of the gut, which can be fatal.

- When you add new bedding, pile it up in the middle of the cage. This way your hamsters can be occupied as they arrange their home to their own satisfaction.

- You may want to provide your hamsters with an even deeper area to burrow in. An area with a solid floor filled with deep bedding has been shown by scientists to be very important to hamster welfare. If the whole cage is not suitable then provide them with a large, deep plastic box as a digging pit in part of their accommodation. Fill the box with a mixture of sand and soil. The sand should be the type used for children's sandpits and the soil sterilised. This is easily done by heating it in a microwave, but make sure it is completely cool before you put it in your hamster's digging pit. You will need to provide a ramp so your hamster can get in and out of the box easily!

- Attach a water bottle to the side of the cage. A bottle is better than a bowl as water bowls can quickly be soiled with food and bedding, or be tipped over, making your hamster's home damp.

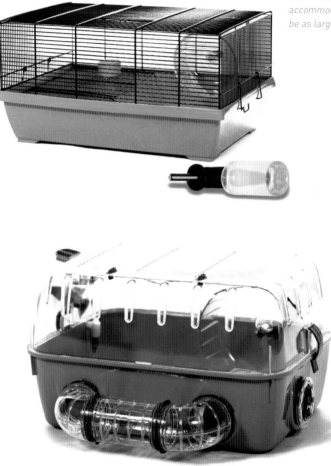

Your hamster's accommodation should be as large as possible.

- Hamsters are clean animals, and can easily be toilet trained. Your hamster will choose the part of its home it thinks suitable as a toilet area for urinating. You will know where this is by the soiled bedding or by the white crust formed from the dried urine. In this spot, place a jam jar on its side with some clean bedding and a little soiled bedding in it. This tells the hamster that this is its new toilet. The jar should be cleaned regularly, at least weekly, and replaced as necessary.

- Ensure your hamster's home is safe from other pets and that he has plenty of places to hide if he is scared.

  When you take your hamster out of the cage do be very careful – hamsters are quick to escape and not easy to recapture!

- You should have a dedicated play-pen that is blocked off so that your hamsters cannot escape under the furniture, or floor boards! The play-pen area should have a dark box or tunnel that your hamster can use as a safe hiding place. Small pet play-pens are available in many pet stores.

Pictured: Handle your hamster carefully when removing it from or returning it to, the cage.

Playtime

Dwarf hamsters should be given the chance to behave naturally where play is concerned. They are inquisitive animals and in the wild would tunnel through the grass, climb over rocks, dig burrows and forage for food.

All hamsters should be given lots of bedding and appropriate toys to play with, to give them both physical and mental stimulation. Give them toys made of natural, untreated wood. Wooden toys made for parrots are suitable, and a twig from a fruit tree is ideal.

Do not give hard,plastic toys that can splinter and leave sharp edges.

You may even wish to teach your dwarf hamster tricks, which can be a great way of bonding and is lots of fun (see further reading). They can be taught to come when called, go back to their cage on cue, and even retrieve tiny objects.

You can help your hamster to live a full life by doing the following:

- Make hiding places from cardboard boxes or the cardboard centres of toilet rolls. These can be empty or you can put bedding and food in them, giving your pet the chance to rummage for tasty treats and chew up the cardboard box – real hamster heaven.

Hamsters are agile, inquisitive and playful and love new toys and challenges.

- Provide your hamster with a wheel. This should have a solid back and sides, but not an exposed spindle. It should fit to the side of the cage. An alternative is the 'flying saucer' wheel that is free standing, slightly dish-shaped and tilted at a 45° angle. Be careful not get one that is too small.

- Get your hamster an exercise ball, also known as a globe ball. This is a plastic ball into which you put the hamster and it can move the ball around the room. But such play should be supervised at all times.

Pictured opposite: A solid wheel is one way your hamster can exercise, but also provide toys and different levels in the cage to encourage climbing and investigating.

Where do I get my dwarf hamster from?

There should be a wide variety of dwarf hamsters available at your local pet store. They should, ideally be kept in spacious runs to give you the opportunity to watch them and make your choice.

You could consider giving unwanted hamsters a new home. Many pet stores now have adoption centres and of course there are many associations that are constantly looking to re-home unwanted pets.

If you are interested in a particular variety, then you may wish to get your hamsters from a reputable breeder.

Pictured: Bright clear eyes and a clean coat are indications of a healthy hamster.

Signs of a healthy hamster

Check that the hamsters you choose are fit and well. A reputable pet store or breeder should be able to tell you all about the hamsters in their care.

You might want to ask about the following questions:

How old is the hamster?

Ideally it should be around 5 – 6 weeks old. Older animals are fine, if they have been handled and are tame.

At what age to you get hamsters into your shop?

A good pet shop should never get animals that are less than 4 weeks old as they are still dependent on their mother for milk.

Have they been treated for any illness?

Clearly they should be fit and well. If, however, the answer is yes, then you need to know what for. If the hamster has had treatment for its teeth, skin or for wet tail (see health section) then you may want to reconsider getting this particular hamster. It may have ongoing or other health issues which will need further veterinary care. Superficial wounds or abrasions are of less concern if they have been properly treated and the hamster has been passed as healthy by the store or the breeder's vet.

What food is it being fed?

You should keep to the existing diet when you take your dwarf hamster home as sudden changes can cause digestive problems. You may wish to change the diet, but this should be done gradually over a couple of weeks.

Ask the shop assistant to get the dwarf hamster out for you to gently handle and check. The following list will give you an idea of what to look for.

Body

The body should be rounded and plump (not fat), with a straight spine and strong well-muscled hips and shoulders.

Coat & skin

The coat should be clean and not greasy, with no bald spots. Check the skin for dry scaly patches, wounds, lumps or swellings. There should be none. Lumps and swellings may mean the hamster has an abscess which will need veterinary treatment.

Hamster skin is loose fitting, rather like it is wearing a coat that is a size too big. If you gently pinch it, it should quickly go back into shape. If, however, it stays erect then it is a sign that the hamster is dehydrated.

Eyes

Look for bright, clear eyes, with no dry discharge or weeping. These signs indicate that the hamster may have conjunctivitis or something in its eye. Cloudy eyes also indicate that there may be an infection.

Ears

There should be no sign of damage on the outer ear, and the ears should be clean with no discharge or waxy build-up.

Nose

This too should be clean, with no signs of discharge, mucous or any crusty residue.

Teeth

Healthy hamster teeth should be a creamy yellow colour, though they become a darker yellow with age. The top and bottom front teeth (two on the top and two on the bottom) should be straight, meet snugly, and not be mis-aligned or broken.

Feet

There should be 4 toes on the front feet and 5 on the back. The underside of the feet should be clean with no wounds or thick, scaly skin.

Bottom

Check the hamster's rump for any soiling, which could indicate diarrhoea. If the area looks greasy then it may be suffering from wet tail.

Pictured: A healthy alert dwarf hamster, with new born babies. Note the 4 toes on the feet.

Movement

Look for free movement; there should be no sign of lameness.

Sexing

You can tell the sex of your hamster by looking under its rear end. Males are sexually mature around 4-5 weeks of age and will have a lump where the testicles are. It is normal for these to be quite large in hamsters. Younger animals can be identified as male or female by the distance between the anus and the genitalia. In females the two are close together, while in males there is a noticeable gap.

Sexing hamsters correctly will avoid unwanted litters.

Making friends

Though hamsters are naturally curious animals, they are easily frightened and will be anxious when they first come to live with you in their new home. If you spend time getting to know your hamsters, they will stop being frightened of you and become very tame.

For the first couple of days, your hamsters need peace and quiet to settle into their new home. You will need to provide food and change the water, so they can start getting used to you, without the stress of being handled. You can even train them to come to you when called. Start this by whistling or saying his name softly, and tap on the cage gently before you put the food down. He will soon learn that your voice and his name mean something pleasant.

Ideally buy hamsters that are already bonded.

Handling

Hamsters naturally wake up around dusk and go back to sleep around dawn. They are most active after dark, which is not always in tune with their owner's routine. You can teach your hamsters to get used to getting up a bit earlier, in the late afternoon or early evening, by waking them at the same time every day for their petting, grooming and playtime.

Remember that hamsters do find bright light painful, so you may need to draw the curtains and put on sidelights if it is very light outside. If your hamsters are asleep, then do wake them gently. Just as with humans, if you wake your hamsters suddenly they will be disorientated, stressed and rather fearful and may bite you as they do not realise who you are. Wake your hamsters gently by talking to them and gently rustling their bedding with your finger or a pencil. Once awake, give them a minute or two to get their bearings before you try to handle them.

Encouraging contact with food rewards the hamster for his efforts, and he feels safer as you handle him. But use small pieces of food, rather than a whole carrot!

When your hamsters appear to be awake, happy and relaxed, you can start making friends.

- To begin with, come close to the cage and talk to them. Do not make any sudden movements that will alarm them.

- Offer treats so the hamsters have to come up to see you and get used to your hand. Hold your hand quite still and let the hamsters sniff your fingers. If you move suddenly you are likely to scare them and may get nipped if they panic.

- The next stage is to put some food on the palm of your open hand and let your hamsters walk on to your hand to get the treat. When they are happy to do this, gently place your other hand over the

Hold your hand quite still and let your hamsters sniff your fingers.

hamster's back, lift him out of the cage and bring him to your chest. This way you will not make your hamster scared of you and your hand. Only pick up one hamster at a time.

Let your hamster walk on to your hand when he feels it is safe to do so.

- Use the same technique to put each hamster back in the cage.

- Do not scoop or grab your dwarf hamster from above. From the hamster's point of view this sudden movement means he is being attacked by a predator, so he will be very frightened and is highly likely to bite you.

- Likewise, do not hold your hamster by the loose skin at the scruff of his neck. This is painful, and again the hamster will tell you by biting. He can wriggle and is very agile, so he can turn and get hold of your fingers. Dwarf hamsters may be small but they can bite hard! If the Hamster is being handled by a young child, make sure you supervise.

Do not turn your hamster on his back and stroke his tummy. He will lie very still, because this is a very scary position for him, and he will play dead, to escape the attentions of an imaginary predator.

This is a common behaviour in many small animals. Do not be fooled into thinking that your hamster is relaxed or in a trance. Research has shown that he is very alert and stressed. When he thinks it is safe to do so, he will suddenly try to escape and may injure himself.

Always handle your hamsters over a table or near the floor in case they accidentally fall out of your hands. Their bones are tiny and easily broken.

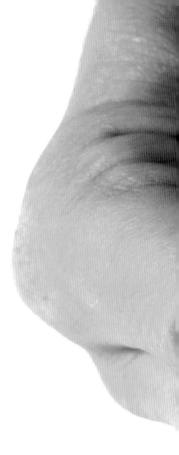

Hold your hamster gently in a safe 'burrow' in your hand. Do not scoop him up from above, he will be scared as this is what a predator would do.

If you have other pets, such as a dog, cat or ferret, you will need to be very careful. You should never allow other pets near without supervision. Dog, cats, ferrets and snakes are meat-eaters and you would not want your hamsters to end up as their tasty snack.

Always make sure your hamster is safe. Dogs and cats are predators and will view your hamster as prey.

Food glorious food

A well-balanced diet will keep your Dwarf hamster healthy, and will help to ensure a good, long life. In the wild, they eat grass, plants, roots, seeds, berries and insects, and will even eat meat if they find a carcase. It is essential that they eat a lot of hard foods that help keep their teeth in good shape.

Complete foods

There are several varieties of hamster food available in pet shops. Some are mixes that look a bit like human muesli; others are pellets or blocks.

Mixes

These are particularly enjoyable for hamsters as they can nibble at different bits as their fancy takes them. Do check your pet's hoard of food every week. If it is too big it means you are feeding too much, and your hamster may only be eating his favourite bits and not getting a balanced diet.

Be careful of buying cheap brands, as these may not have the correct proportions of protein and fats for your pet, or contain mixed animal protein rather than from a particular type of animal. A good mix will contain seeds, nuts, dried fruit and grains and some animal protein (usually chicken). They may come pre-packed or loose in bins so you can take the amount you require. Do not buy food that has lots of raisins and fruit in it as these can cause digestive problems such as diarrhoea. Also, the high sugar content of the fruit can lead to dental disease and obesity.

Pellet or nugget food

These are hard blocks of food with all the ingredients needed packed into one chunk. This means the hamster cannot choose to feed selectively. This type of food is less common nowadays and has been replaced by mixes.

Fresh food

Hamsters need to have fresh food once or twice a week at least. Remember you do not need to give much, the equivalent of an inch or so (2-3 cm) of dandelion leaf or a thin slice of carrot is plenty. Fresh herbs, such as parsley, grass, clover and dandelion, bits of apple, carrot, broccoli or grape will be much appreciated.

Avoid giving your hamster citrus fruits as these can cause mouth sores. Lettuce, spinach, buttercups, privet, ragwort, bluebells and pineapple should not be given to your hamster, nor any ornamental plants or flowers. Do not feed grass cuttings from a lawn mower, but picked grass only.

When giving any fresh food to your pet it is important to make sure it is rinsed well under cold water to clean away any dirt. You should never feed any fruit or vegetable that is over or under-ripe or that is wilting, as this is not healthy for your hamster. A good rule of thumb to follow is: would you eat it? If not then do not feed it to your pet.

Never collect fresh plants from the side of the road or from areas that have been, or are likely to have been, sprayed with pesticides as this will cause harm to your hamster.

Meat

Hamsters are omnivores so they eat meat and vegetables, and need meat protein in their diet. This is already in the better commercial diets, but your hamster will enjoy a little bird 'insect food' added to his dinner, the occasional mealworm, a small piece of plain, cooked chicken and even a small bit of boiled or scrambled egg.

Only give a very small amount of fresh food and meat at a time. If you give too much and your hamsters hoard it away it will quickly go bad and may cause your pets to become ill.

Treats

Pet stores now sell a range of treats for dwarf hamsters. The best ones are those that contain natural ingredients. Some can be hidden in their bedding, or hanging sticks and sprays of millet (often used for budgies) can be attached to the cage bars.

Do not give your pets human chocolate, crisps or salted nuts as these are very harmful to hamsters. Pet shops sell special pet chocolate and yogurt drops. These should be given very sparingly, as should treats that are covered in honey or sticky sweet coatings. Dwarf hamsters can suffer from painful dental problems and can also can get fat, risking heart disease or diabetes.

A treat is a treat, not part of the hamster's normal daily diet. Use them when you are playing with, or training, your hamster as a way to bond with him.

How much?

It is normal for a hamster to hoard excess food, but if this hoard is large you are feeding your pet too much. It is suggested in the next section that you regularly weigh your hamsters to ensure they are not putting on weight. If they are putting on weight then you are feeding either too much of their normal diet, or, more likely, too many sugary treats.

Hamster care

Looking after your hamsters means you need to keep their home clean and be alert to health problems.

Cleaning out the cage might not be the most fun aspect of owning hamsters, but it is very rewarding when you watch your pets enjoy their freshly clean, comfortable surroundings and make their new beds. If the hamsters are pets for a child, then remember, an adult must ensure they are properly fed and the cage cleaned. It is important that an adult does the routine weekly health checks, alongside the child, to ensure nothing is missed.

Hamsters are naturally extremely clean animals. They keep their home very tidy, remaking their bed every day by moving out any soiled bedding, and they also check their food stores to remove any food that is decomposing. In addition, a hamster leaves a scent around his home. This acts as a territory marker, defining its property and making it feel safe, as well as warning others that they are entering its home.

Do not overfeed and remember to remove any decomposing food.

These fastidious hamster habits mean that the cage only needs to be lightly cleaned on a weekly basis with a more thorough clean every month.

Daily tasks

- Refill the water-bottle with fresh water, and make sure it is low enough for your hamster to reach without the nozzle end touching the bedding.

- Remove any wet bedding.

- Handle your hamsters and give them an opportunity to explore their play pen or exercise ball, and maybe do some training.

- Check your hamsters' bottoms to ensure they are clean.

See the 'Health' section for more information.

Make sure your dwarf hamster can reach the water bottle easily.

Weekly tasks

- Confine your hamsters to a second holding cage, play pen or exercise ball – somewhere where they will be safe while you clean out the cage.

- Remove all the toys, bowls and other objects in the cage.

- Remove all bedding and put some of it to one side. Throw the rest away.

Brush the cage out thoroughly with a stiff cleaning brush, and then give the floor of the cage a light spray with an 'animal friendly' disinfectant. Do not use any household cleaning products, as these may be toxic to your hamsters.

Put in the new bedding and the bit of old bedding that you kept to one side. This means your hamsters will feel safer when you return them to their home as they will have a familiar scent.

- Clean and fill the water bottle.

- Give all your hamsters an all-over health check – see Health section.

- Weigh each hamster to check it is not losing or gaining weight. Use household cooking scales for this, but do make sure your hamster does not fall out of the scale dish.

Monthly tasks

Once a month it is worth giving your hamsters' cage a full clean. Follow the routine as described for the weekly clean, but wash down all the bars, shelving and your hamsters' 'sleeping houses' in a disinfectant especially for cages of small animals. Then rinse thoroughly with clean warm water. Do make sure everything is completely dry before putting in the new bedding (and some old bedding) and returning your hamsters to their home.

A full clean of the cage once a month is a good idea.

Grooming

The amount of grooming each hamster needs depends on coat length. All hamsters can be groomed weekly. Long-haired hamsters will need to be brushed more frequently to ensure the fur does not get tangled and matted. Grooming is a good way of bonding with your pet and helps keep the coat and underlying skin healthy. It also enables you to check for any problems. Hamsters will groom themselves with great enthusiasm and are so flexible that they can reach all of their body. As hamsters get old they may become stiff and will appreciate some gentle assistance in keeping their coat in tip-top condition.

A healthy hamster's coat will look well groomed.

There are several suitable brushes that can be used for your hamster, including a finger brush. This is a small rubber brush that fits on your finger like a thimble. Always brush the coat in the direction the hair lays.

Even long-haired dwarf hamsters do not have very long hair, but if your hamster should get knots in its hair, ensure you hold the hair below the knot and gently ease the knot with small flicks of the brush. Do not tug, wrench or pull too hard or you may pull the hair out from the skin or even tear the skin. If the knot or tangle is not being moved easily, cut it away with a pair of curved surgical scissors. This needs to be done VERY carefully as hamsters can wriggle and squirm and it is very easy to cut the skin underneath. If in doubt contact your vet or an experienced hamster owner who may be able to do this for you.

Start grooming, as with handling, from an early age, perhaps when the hamster is enjoying a tasty treat, so that he learns to relax and enjoy the attention.

A hamster that has been gently handled since he was young will be a very rewarding companion.

Bathing

You should only bath your hamster if it is absolutely necessary – if his coat is very sticky, for example. Dwarf hamsters lose heat very rapidly because of their size and if wet they may quickly develop a dangerously low body temperature. Most hamsters will never need a bath, and you certainly should NEVER give them one just for fun.

Bathing your hamster will be a very stressful experience for your pet. If you do need to do it you will require a plastic bowl, a very soft, small hand towel, small animal shampoo, (available from your pet shop) and a bowl of clean, tepid water to use to rinse your pet. Put a small amount of cool, tepid water, (not cold) in the bowl. Remember not to make the water hot. You only need enough to cover your hamster's legs. Gently put your hamster in the water and cup it with one hand. Lightly flick water over it with the other, avoiding the nose and eyes.

Once the coat is wet, gently massage in a small amount of the shampoo using a finger, but avoid the head, eyes and ears. Then you will need to rinse your pet's coat using the water in which it is standing and a final rinse or two with the clean water in the other bowl. Follow the same method as when you started to wet the coat. Rinse the coat clean, so all the soap suds have gone and the water runs clear.

You now need to dry your hamster. Do this using a soft towel and the tips of your fingers. Be very gentle, but do make sure your pet is completely dry. Expect to get bitten!! Having a bath is not an experience your hamster will enjoy.

Finally, return your hamster to his cage, making sure there is lots of bedding for him to snuggle into and that the cage is in a warm room. Then leave him alone. Your hamster will have been extremely stressed and needs time to recover from the bathing ordeal.

Your hamster should never need a bath.

Hamster behaviour

One of the most rewarding things about owning a pet is learning to understand what it is thinking or feeling. You can learn a lot about what your hamster is saying to you by listening to the sounds it makes and observing his body postures.

Listen to your hamster

Hamsters make few noises that we can hear. They do make sounds in the ultrasonic range, 20– 60 KHz, but this is way beyond our hearing. However, there are a few sounds you may hear your hamster make.

Gnawing hard foods like peanuts in the shell is fun and good for teeth.

Cackle

This is the sound that hamsters use when they are defending their home. Usually this is only made when they see another hamster, but if your pet is worried it may use the same noise to tell you it wants to be left alone.

Teeth chattering

Again, this sound means 'go away', and is usually used by males. If the other animal does not go away, fighting is likely to ensue.

Squawk

If your hamster squawks it is telling you it is either very frightened or in pain!

Screeching

Dwarf hamsters that are in a fierce fight will make loud screeching noises. They also do this when they are trying to defend themselves from a predator. Baby hamsters that are disturbed in the nest will roll on their backs and start screeching in a concerted effort to frighten the predator away.

Squeaking

Dwarf hamsters will make soft, squeaking noises to each other.

Make sure the hamster's wheel has a solid floor and is the right size.

Watch your hamster

Scent rubbing

Being an animal that is active in the dark, a main form of hamster communication is through scent – smells that humans are unable to detect, let alone interpret. However, they clearly mean a lot to your hamsters and you can watch them leaving messages all over the place. The three short tailed (Phodopus) species have scent glands on their belly and will press their belly to the ground to leave a scent mark.

Chinese hamsters have scent glands on both flanks and they will arch their back and rub their flank on the walls of their cage and other vertical surfaces. They will also roll on their side to leave scent on the ground and on objects in the cage.

I'm watching you! But you also need to watch for changes in your hamster's behaviour; it could save his life.

Happy hamster

Inquisitive

When your dwarf hamster is curious he will stand up on his back legs, with his front paws relaxed and drooping. It may have been a sound or a smell that caught your hamster's attention, such as your arrival, and he will turn to face the direction of your approach. He may even climb up onto something so he can be a bit higher and thus see, hear and smell even better.

Curious but cautious

Hamsters are curious creatures, but sensibly they are also cautious about any new thing they come across.

When your hamster is investigating his world he will walk with a staggered gait that is made up of small, stiff movements while rocking back and forth, ready to run if need be.

Annoyed hamster

Sitting back and 'Bearing'

A hamster that is sitting back on his hind legs looking like a miniature bear (hence the name of this position) may look like he is smiling and ready for a game, with his mouth wide open and teeth pointed forward. In fact, he is saying the direct opposite! This position is a hamster's way of saying 'leave me alone or I will attack'.

Ears pinned back

If your hamster's ears are pinned back against his head, he is saying he wishes to be left alone. This is the usual position of the ears when the hamster is asleep... It is his 'Do not disturb' sign! If you wake your hamster, wait until those ears are upright and your pet is fully awake and ready to interact with you.

Frightened hamster

Freezing

When a hamster suddenly stops what he is doing and 'freezes on the spot' it means he has heard, seen or smelled something unusual and scary. He is frightened. This is usually followed by running back to a safe shelter.

Playing dead

If your hamster lies absolutely still, usually on his back, he is extremely frightened. Your hamster is trying to pretend to be dead and thus of no interest to a predator. He will remain like this until the scary thing has gone away. This is a common behaviour in many small animals, including rabbits, and used in what they perceive to be a life-or-death situation. Do not be fooled and think your hamster is in a trance or is relaxed. Scientists have shown that they are very alert and stressed.

If you see your hamster do this, leave him alone for 24 hours to recover. Think about what might have caused him to have been so very, very frightened. It may have been a loud noise, a sudden bright light, or being chased and grabbed. Try and take steps to avoid the situation occurring again.

Rolling on its back

If you startle your pet, for example by trying to pick
him up when he is not fully awake, he will roll over on
its back and kick and bite. While freezing and running
away is the hamster's main form of self-defence, if
he has been caught unawares, or has nowhere to run
to, kicking and biting is his way of defending himself
from what he perceives as a danger.

Grooming each other

Hamsters that are happy in each other's company
will gently nibble and groom each other's fur. This is
known as 'allogrooming'.

Unhappy hamster

Bar gnawing

You may see your hamster repeatedly gnawing at the bars of his cage, often for long periods at a time. This behaviour is a sign of an animal that is stressed, and a hamster may be so stressed that it does not stop even if he has made his nose and mouth sore, or damaged his teeth.

The common cause of this behaviour is boredom, meaning the hamster does not have enough space and / or things to do, or anywhere to escape from the unwanted attentions of the other hamsters in the cage. Other causes include the cage being in a part of the house that is too brightly lit or too noisy. Remember, that does not simply mean the noise that you and I can hear, but ultrasonic noise, such as from refrigerators.

You should try giving your pets more space, hiding places and things to do. Think carefully whether you have put the cage in the most suitable place.

This hamster is actually grooming, but looks like he is covering his ears. Remember your hamster has very acute hearing, is sensitive to noises, and needs a peaceful home.

Health

Healthy hamsters can live up to two years. Handling your pet every day and performing regular health checks will help you pick up on the early signs of ill health. This is best done while handling your pet in the normal way. You should make any examinations as part of your grooming and regular play.

Weigh your hamster on a regular basis and remember to keep a record of its weight. Weight loss is often the first sign of ill health in a hamster.

You should know how your pet behaves while healthy. A sudden change in his normal pattern of behaviour can also indicate ill health, such as a change in eating habits, hiding more, or becoming aggressive.

Hamsters are prey animals and are very good at disguising signs of illness and pain, so familiarity with your own pet is vital. It is important that you contact a vet as soon as possible if you have any concerns about your hamster's health.

Hamsters are very caring mothers, but must not be disturbed when they have young babies.

Going to the vet

If you have two or more hamsters living together, it is best to take them all to the vet at the same time, if you can. This is for two reasons. Firstly, if one Hamster is ill, it is a good idea to get all the group checked out. Secondly, hamsters identify each other by smell and if they have been separated may not recognise each other when put back together, and may squabble and fight. This is quite likely if one has gone to the vet and comes back with a different scent.

If you do have to separate them, spend a couple of days putting some used bedding from each cage into that of the other animal's before putting them back together. It is a good idea to wipe a clean cloth over one hamster and then over the other, and then do the same the other way round with a second clean cloth. This will help each hamster smell of the other, a process called scent swapping, and thus be more likely to recognise and accept each other as friends when they are reintroduced.

Smell is an important way of detecting danger... or your approach with tasty foodstuffs.

Common hamster ailments

This section gives some of the more common problems that dwarf hamsters can suffer from. Accidents, injuries or illness may occur and in the first instance a vet should be contacted to arrange treatment. But, in the time between the discovery of a problem and reaching the surgery you are responsible for providing the best care you can.

Hamsters hide illness well, and will often go quiet and hide away when unwell.

Wounds & mishaps

Because hamsters are active, inquisitive, short-sighted and so easily frightened, they may get injured when investigating their world or when trying to run away from something that has scared them.

Stress is often the underlying cause of wounds and bald patches on the nose, or around the lips. These can become inflamed, red or even bleed, due to bar rubbing. Your pet should be seen by the vet, and you should consider what may be causing the problem.

Most minor grazes can be treated by being gently cleaned, using a cotton bud dipped in salty water (tap water and rock salt, 6 g (1 teaspoon) of salt in half a litre (1 pint) of lukewarm water). However, more serious injuries such as cuts must be looked at and treated by a veterinary surgeon as soon as possible to prevent infection and abscesses. Try and keep the wound as clean as possible until you go to the vet.

While they are usually peaceful, dwarf hamsters can and do fight, especially if they have been separated, or two males clash over a female. The Chinese hamster is the most aggressive of the four species, and it is because of this that it is generally advised that they are kept on their own. Female Chinese hamsters tend to win in fights with males and will often leave the male with nasty bites on his rump and scrotum. If this happens, the male needs to be taken to the vet.

Bite wounds generally heal quite quickly, as long as they are not too big or deep, in which case they will need veterinary treatment. Clean small bites as described above. Remove all sand or sawdust from the cage for a few days to avoid infecting the wound. Give the hamsters extra shredded paper or shredded kitchen roll instead.

Broken bones

One of the main reasons hamsters have to be handled so carefully is that they have very fine bones which can easily fracture, including the skull. Blood in the nose or ears, could mean your pet has hurt his head badly. If you believe your pet has a broken bone, phone your vet immediately. The same applies if you see blood in the urine. Your vet may advise you to bring your dwarf hamster in as soon as possible for stabilisation and pain relief. In the meantime, keep him in a darkened and quiet area. He will feel safer and more relaxed in a dark enclosed space, such as a travelling box lined with soft bedding.

Teeth

Keep a close check on your hamster's teeth to make sure they do not grow too long or are mis-aligned. This can indicate a variety of possible problems including inadequate diet, fractured teeth from a fall, abscesses or some other illness. If your hamster is having difficulty eating (this is one reason to check his weight weekly), you need to take him to the vet. Be warned, overgrown teeth can lead to serious and even fatal problems for hamsters. The chance of your pet developing tooth problems is greatly reduced if he is fed correctly and has lots of suitable toys.

A good, balanced diet will help prevent teeth and bone problems.

Nails

In the wild, a hamster keeps his nails in trim by running and digging. A pet hamster's nails may grow too long, which will make moving very uncomfortable as the nails can curve over and dig into the bottom of the feet.

Providing your hamsters with a digging pit will help keep nails in good condition. You could also put some rough surfaces in the cage, such as a couple of bricks, for your hamsters to climb over.

If your hamster's nails are getting overgrown they will need to be trimmed. It is advised that you have them trimmed by the vet or an experienced hamster keeper who has done the task before.

Trimming hamster nails is very fiddly as the nails are very small and it is extremely easy to cut or even break the hamster's toe or cut the nail too short, down to the quick or nail-bed. The nail bed is pink coloured as it contains blood vessels and nerves. While easy to see on light coloured nails, if your hamster has dark nails it can be difficult to judge where the quick is. In that case, trim the nails to the same length as any white ones your hamster has, or just remove the tip.

Cutting the nail-bed is very painful and will probably bleed. If this happens, dip the toe into some wound powder made specifically for small animals; or put a blob of Vaseline or even flour on the end of the wounded nail to seal it. If you cut the quick or think you have damaged a toe, your hamster will be in shock and will need to be kept warm. Wrap it in a soft piece of towel – a large, thick, dry facecloth is ideal – and seek veterinary help.

Untreated wood is good, for climbing and gnawing!

Bumble foot

This is an extremely painful condition and is
characterised by the feet becoming swollen and
blistered, which can turn into open pressure sores.
The infection can spread to the bones of the feet and
if you see such signs on the feet of your hamster
then you must take it to the vet as soon as you can.
If you do not, your hamster may have to have his foot
amputated or may die of blood poisoning.

A major cause of bumble foot is keeping
hamsters on mesh floors rather than
flat floors, or on damp,
dirty bedding.

Wet tail

This is a secondary bacterial infection that occurs and takes hold when the dwarf hamster is already unwell. It is commonly triggered by stress – for example, transportation to the shop or new home, or excessive handling before he has settled in. Another cause is diet, typically too much fruit and vegetables.

Wet tail causes serious diarrhoea and the hamster can rapidly dehydrate, causing life-threatening loss of fluids and salts. The obvious symptoms are clumped greasy hair around the rump area with a strong sickly-sweet smell. The hamster will become very lethargic and withdrawn, and the rest of his coat will look and feel greasy and stand on end.

In the later stages, the hamster's eyes look dull and sunken and the skin looses its elasticity. Such a degree of dehydration may cause further problems, such as kidney disease. All this can happen very quickly. The first 24 hours are the most important, so getting veterinary treatment is vital in the early stages.

As this is a very infectious disease, all the hamsters in the cage need to be taken to the veterinary surgeon.

Cleanliness is extremely important. Completely clean the cage at once, and replace all bedding materials.

Remove your pet's toys to reduce the places that the bacteria may grow. It may help to put a little millet spray and chopped peanuts into a food bowl with a little 'canary egg food' to help thicken up the stools. Sick hamsters may be so weakened that they will not drink from their bottle, so put a little juicy cucumber in the cage for them to nibble.

Hair loss

If your hamster has hair loss and is scratching a lot, seemingly incessantly, then he probably has a parasite infestation such as skin mites.

Bald patches can also indicate further problems, particularly if your hamster is not scratching a lot. These non-itchy bald patches may be a sign that your hamster has a tumour or skin cancer.

Whether itchy or not, take your hamster to the vet, along with any others with whom he shares a cage, as skin mites are infectious.

Impacted pouches/ facial lumps

Sometimes hamsters try to put too much into their pouches or they struggle to remove items in them. Most commonly this is bedding material. This will have to be removed by you, an experienced hamster handler or a vet. If, after closer examination, it is not the cheek pouches that are causing the swelling it may be a tooth abscess or a tumour. This will need urgent veterinary treatment.

Appearing dead/ hibernation

In the wild a hamster will hibernate during colder weather. If the ambient temperature falls to around 5°C (41°F) or lower then the hamster may enter a state of hibernation. With central heating it is unusual for the room temperature to fall so low, but it can still happen.

If you think that your hamster is hibernating, place it on a warm towel in an open top deep box, in his cage, so he cannot accidentally get out and get lost. Put him into an airing cupboard or warm room where he can gently come round. Check on your hamster periodically to ensure all is well.

If your hamster is sluggish and unresponsive and has not been exposed to cold, then he is ill and you should seek veterinary advice.

Twirling

This is when a hamster repeatedly spins or walks in circles. If seen in a very young hamster it is possible he had brain damage from birth. In older animals, it may be the result of a middle ear infection or brain damage from a stroke or tumour.

Like bar biting, it can also be a behaviour that indicates a psychological problem, namely a stressed or bored hamster.

Tyzzer's disease

This is a bacterial disease that can be a problem in large breeding colonies. The symptoms are very similar to that of wet tail, but are found predominantly in the weaning young. They are due to stress, including overcrowding. It should not, therefore, be seen in your pet hamster, especially if you have brought him from a responsible breeder or pet shop that has given their young hamsters a health check.

To reiterate, if you wish to breed your hamsters you will need to do further research about the needs of breeding animals and their young. Do remember you will be responsible for their health and welfare, and for homing the babies.

Unless you are very committed, breeding dwarf hamsters is not recommended. Instead, enjoy the company of your unique, special, furry, comical hamster friends in single sex groups, or, in the case of Chinese hamsters, on their own.

Hamster medicine

Veterinary knowledge of hamsters has increased hugely over the last few years and there is much more that can be done for your pet. However, unlike cat and dog medicine, which all veterinary surgeons know a lot about, hamsters are a specialist subject and it is worth finding a vet who is interested in hamsters and their treatment.

Know your dwarf hamster

Winter White Russian or Siberian Winter White

Scientific name	Phodopus sungorus sungorus
Group order	Rodentia
Genus	Short tailed dwarf hamsters- Phodopus
Sexually mature	Males 3- 4 weeks; Females 3- 4 weeks
Gestation	18-20 days
Litter size	6- 7
Birth weight	1.4 g (0.05 oz)
Birth type	hairless, ears and eyes closed
Eyes open	14 days
Weaning	21- 28 days
Adult weight	21- 24 g (0.7- 0.8 oz)
Adult length	body: 67-100 mm (2.6- 3.9 inches); tail: 6-15 mm (0.2- 0.6 inches)
Feet	Furry soles
Dorsal Stripe	Yes

Campbell's Russian

Scientific name	Phodopus sungorus campbellii
Group order	Rodentia
Genus	Short tailed dwarf hamsters- Phodopus
Sexually mature	Males 3- 4 weeks; Females 3- 4 weeks
Gestation	16-18 days
Litter size	5- 6
Birth weight	1.8 g (0.06 oz)
Birth type	hairless, ears and eyes closed
Eyes open	14 days
Weaning	21- 28 days
Adult weight	30- 50 g (1- 1.7 oz)
Adult length	body: 70- 110 mm (2.8- 4.3 inches); tail: 6- 18 mm (0.2- 0.7 inches)
Feet	Furry soles
Dorsal Stripe	Yes

Roborovski

Scientific name	Phodopus roborovskii
Group order	Rodentia
Genus	Short tailed dwarf hamsters- Phodopus
Sexually mature	Males 3- 4 weeks; Females 3- 4 weeks
Gestation	20- 22 days
Litter size	4
Birth weight	1.2 g (0.04 oz)
Birth type	hairless, ears and eyes closed
Eyes open	14 days
Weaning	21- 28 days
Adult weight	20- 25 g (0.7- 0.9 oz)
Adult length	body: 68- 92 mm (2.7- 3.6 inches); tail: 6-12 mm (0.2- 0.5 inches)
Feet	bare soles
Dorsal Stripe	No

Chinese

Scientific name	Cricetulus griseus
Group order	Rodentia
Genus	Long tailed dwarf hamsters - Cricetulus
Sexually mature	Males 3-4 weeks; Females 3-4 weeks
Gestation	20 - 22 days
Litter size	7
Birth weight	1.7 g (0.06 oz)
Birth type	hairless, ears and eyes closed
Eyes open	14 days
Weaning	21 - 28 days
Adult weight	30 - 45 g (1.05 – 1.6 oz)
Adult length	body: 82 – 127 mm (3.2 – 5 inches); tail: 20-33 mm (0.8 – 1.3 inches)
Feet	bare soles
Dorsal Stripe	Yes

Sources of further information

Orr, J and Lewin, T 2005 Getting Started: clicking with your rabbit. Karen Pryor Publications. Gives excellent advice on how to train rabbits... which can also be applied to hamsters

Websites

www.clickerbunny.com/clickercritterarticles.html Further information on training your hamster and other small pets.

http://www.hamsters-uk.org The National Hamster Club of the UK welcomes members from around the world.

Weights & measures

If you prefer your units in pounds and inches, you can use this conversion chart:

Length in inches	Length in cm	Weight in kg	Weight in lb
1	2.5	0.5	1.1
2	5.1	0.7	1.5
3	7.6	1	2.2
4	10.2	1.5	3.3
5	12.7	2	4.4
8	20.3	3	6.6
10	25.4	4	8.8
15	38.1	5	11

Measurements rounded to 1 decimal place.